NOT ALL ROADS
LEAD TO ROME

NOT ALL ROADS LEAD TO ROME

A Collection of Romantic Poems

Sumit Datta

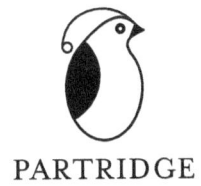

PARTRIDGE

To order additional copies of this book, contact
Partridge India
000 800 10062 62
orders.india@partridgepublishing.com

www.partridgepublishing.com/india

CONTENTS

REMEMBER THOSE DAYS

Remember those days,
Those days of daisy and rose,
Walking under shadows, closer and close.

Those colors and music
Those drops of dews,
Those aromas in air
Those dreams of billion hues.

Life like a twisted river
Carried you to the harbors
Hundred miles away
To the bays of storm,
Islands of green,
Continents of blue.

Your sorrows sailed on sea,
Your mirth spilled on earth,
You gained so much,
You lost so many.

Even then the theatrics of life has left

Nothing for you,

Will leave nothing for you

Except those days

Of sweetest remembrance.

Those days of daisy and rose,

Being together, few moments, closer and close.

LOST AND FOUND

Many rainy days
Rain inside me, when I see
You to drench in rain.

My roses lament,
Scent of my camellia
Roams around my heart.

My wailing meadows
Await for tender footsteps,
My sky turns azure.

It begins to rain
Even though it does not rain,
Winds become insane.

And those rainy days
Come inside me; when I see
You to drench in rain.

MY LIFE WITHOUT YOU

My life without you
Wails in penumbra, like a
Dew drop without hue.

In dense wilderness
Like sorrow stricken sparrow
All my songs die out.

From heart of silence
Foments sentimental tune
And wafts with ballads.

My life without you
Is like a plucked and thrown rose,
Full of blue and rue.

———◆◆◆———

NOT ALL ROADS
LEAD TO ROME

Not all roads lead to Rome,
Some roads roam around
Misty shadows, old huts,
Blue lakes and brown lagoons.
From there it takes turn
With western wind and find
The broken red brick road
Guarded by old palm trees.

The breeze wheezes, the bees buzz,
In the far deep greeneries
Children play their own way,
The yellow hay stalks stand still,
Sound comes from a country hand mill.

Not all roads lead to Rome,
Some roads roam around
Long forgotten fables,
Forsaken lanes of past,

Sparkling fenestras of fantasy,
Fires of deadly desire,
Twinkles of sweetest memories.

Not all roads lead to Rome,
Some roads roam around
The mauve shadows of eremite fig,
Where the innocent eye
Plays hide and seek with innocuous sky,
Through the canopy of foliages
The clouds sculpt the dreams,
Blues fill the eye;
Swirls of butterfly
Whirl around the soul.

Not all roads lead to Rome,
Some roads roam around
Meadows of green,
Vales of brown,
Firmament of blue,
Mountains of amber,
Fountains of silver.

Not all roads lead to Rome,
Some roads roam around
The roaring sea shore,
In splashes of the waves,
Blues of the bays
Where forgotten symbols on
Forlorn seashells wail with sound,
Where the hearts nudge each other,
Breaths share sighs,
Lips share the stories of erosion.

Not all roads lead to Rome,
Some roads roam around
These misty twists of remembrance,
Foggy turns of memories,
Where joy becomes rhyme,
Pain becomes hymn,
Words fail to wail.
And those auras of silence,
Blues of darkness scream with
The yelling eyes of shattered dreams.

Not all roads lead to Rome,
Some roads roam around
The dark blue cavern,
Where with the daisy and dancing bees
The saga of innocuous love rests in peace,
Where in every twist and turn
Brown moss sleeps with fern;

There all roads take its turn
To meet that dark blue cavern,
And from there they never return,
They never return.

———◆◆◆———

ETERNAL YEARN

Muses have crafted her
With all music, color
And poetry.

Her glee trances me
Like a restless bee,
Strings of my heart
Ignite the fire of
Divine desire.

Let the soul burn
In her eternal yearn.

THE FLOWER
OF MIDNIGHT HOUR

The garden is full of flowers,
But I want the one which blossoms in midnight hours,
Which chants the melody of dark,
Drinking the silver star's golden spark.

The garden is full of flowers,
But I want the one which blossoms in midnight hours,
Which knows the alphabet of dew,
Words of petals; its mystic hue,
Which knows the language of rain,
Shades of joy and shadows of pain.

The garden is full flowers,
But I want the one which blossoms in midnight hours,
Which can nudge the treasures hidden beneath
Or kiss the bliss coveted in endless zenith.

MY HEART ACHES

My heart aches,
In the solitude of night
Dream drags me
To the majestic hue,
Which in full moon night
I saw on you.

My heart burns,
To touch the urn
Outpoured with mirth
Of your ecstasy.

My heart pains,
The smile painted on your sorrow
Numbs the sense.

My heart rains,
The darkness tells the story,
You and only you are
My essence.

LOVE LINES - 3

To be entranced by
Your joy, zest and glee
Is the reason for which
Passion germinates in me.

To embrace the grace of your joy
And abyss of your sorrow;
I yearn, I burn,
My heart mourns every night, every morrow.

———◆◆———

A MARVELOUS FACE

Music spills out of the lips,
Aimless air plays unruly games
With her careless hair.

Hidden hue in diamond eye
Touches the blue of my
Unbound sky.

Countless grace in pertinent place,
Who else but God
Can create such a marvelous face?

THE LAST KISS

Your footsteps on my
Throbbing heart,
Drag me towards
This eternal art.

The vineyard whines,
The pines cry,
The clouds wipe out the pain
With endless rain.

This vista makes me insane,
Dizzy and drowsy
In pensive disdain.

O heartless sweetheart,
Remember the southern breeze;
On these unending
Blues and greens
Like the loftiest yet cruel bliss,
You gave me the last and final kiss.

WHIM OF MY DREAM

To walk with you, hand in hand
On these rocks, stone, soil and sand,
And to share the soul's abysmal scream
Is the whim of my deadliest dream.

To embosom you in endless embrace
To drink the wine of your charm and grace,
To touch your soul under sweet sun beam
Is the whim of my deadliest dream.

TRANSFORMATION

Suddenly those roses transformed their hue
When by bliss of luck I met you.
Flux of its fragrance pervaded me,
My nothingness turned to flawless florid glee.

It unfolded the meaning of color or essence of incense,
Its' sincere innocence irked my sedated sense.
The sweet little rose
Told me to hold you so close
That we can see in each other's eye
Love of billion blue sky.

LAMENTS

Tear drops, the melting pearl
From the whirls of the heart
Fall on my hand
Like pebbles on the sand.

Evening's evanescent flowers
Shower the sweetest fragrance,
Muses play on strings of my heart;
Deadliest melancholy flows in my vein.

The blue butterfly kisses me,
The stars chant pristine hymn,
I am dying in want of love
Like a hue less, hopeless dove.

CEASELESS

Those touches ephemeral but
Left countless sweet patches
On mist of memory.

Those opulent kisses
Undulate in my crystal sky
Like blushes below the innocent eye.

Those moments of embrace
Pulsate within vein
Like a stream of pain.

Those moments of walk and dream
Painted in eye
Like ceaseless sun beam.

THE BOND

The bee
Never gets attracted to pollen by the glee.
It knows the language of smell and touch,
It knows the alphabet of honey.

Petals wither,
Pedicels dry,
Pollens reach their niche
Before they die.

The bee
Never gets attracted to pollen by the glee,
Under the brilliant sky
They are bonded by love
By unknown yet eternal tie.

SKY AND EARTH

Sky never remembers the songs of earth
It's gloom or glee, tears or mirth,
Sky never looms down to sand
To touch the blues of lamenting land.

Lamentations and mourns on bay
Splash upon the shore night and day,
Blues of autumns or greens of springs
Never pierce the sky, who ever sings.

When the sweet breeze trudges in vale
It tells the sky, earth's sad tale,
Sky never remembers the songs of earth,
Its gloom or glee, tears or mirth.

Heart of earth erodes in rue,
Blue sprawls all over, no other hue,
Implores implode, knock the door,
Will sky any day kiss the shore?

AN EVENING
OF SERENDIPITY

Even in crowded concerts of life
I find myself deserted;
The incandescence of ecstasy touches
But not penetrates me.
I am permeated by flames of your fire;
Yearn of my burning heart
Reincarnates in hums of bee or
Melancholy of a fathomless sea.

The shadows quiver,
I walk in forest of oak and pine,
Rain drops on me like crystal wine.
The hermit banyan
Stands on the bank of roaring river,
Under its innocent foliages
Swirls of my dream flowered,
It showered upon me countless bliss,
In the guise of pain and lament.

In those ignorant eyes
I saw the epiphany of your love,
Entwining me like a serpentine woodbine.
When was I apart?
Even in those ray less recluses and dejected desolations
I was touching your solacing soul.
But how can I convey
These melodious messages,
These springing prayers to whom,
Who is so close yet so far?
I have never learnt the alphabet of love or
Syllogism of romance.
I never walked with a maiden
In the garden of Eden.

Music spilled over the floor,
Dance and drama filled the panorama.
Vista is full of theatrics.
I know those enticing hands
Put you in the heaven on earth,
But I wanted to plant you
On the earth of heaven.

You gave me a placid glance
Consoling my tumults and torments,
In the candlelight you glow,
I burn.

I know this evening of serendipity
Will never be over in my life.
These songs and drama will
Reincarnate in anonymous dreams.
My wishes will be resurrected as a rose
I will come near your heart even more close.

TYRANNY OF MY DREAMS

Tyranny of my dreams tarnishes my reality,
It uplifts me from the prosaic mundaneness
To the poetic elegance.

Soul mocks the protocols of decorated civility,
Ceremonies of intense rituals,
Clamor of diurnal cravings,
Uproar of mediocre hankerings,
Or outcry of violent catharsis.

The evanescent corporeality can not
Search the shadows of heart
Aroma of aesthetics or colors of art.

Here on this drought of romance
The tiny eyes look at wide and vast
With a chest full of thirst, for the
The orison of sea, the litany of sky,
Chant of the low, hymn of the high.

Celerity of ritualized life
Pendent on the pedicels of plastic flower,
It has no spring or autumn,
It has neither winter nor summer,
It has adopted the revelry of commonplace dins.

The tyranny of my dreams
Tarnishes this reality,
It tides away these barren memories,
Frozen fashions, carnal passions.
It rescues me from this terrestrial roar
To holy waves of heavenly shore.

———◆◆◆———

INVOCATION

The amphitheatre of night
Drenched in moonlight,
The wanton wind trudges
Towards the azure moorland;
Reticent boughs waft,
Sleazy foliages fall on the sand.

Warblers in nocturnal zest
Shamble in their flimsy nest,
Pervasive fragrance of trodden petals
Permeates the quintessence of life.

In these quivering shadows
Flickering star lights, maddening odors
The heart can learn
The language of love;
The countenance of beauty
Or the compendium of soul.

These words of eroded heart
Are nothing but occult evocation

Of a taciturn art,
Allusion of abysmal passion.

We can walk through
These tranquil land,
Eyes on eyes, hands in hand
Civilization failed to civilize
These savage foliages,
This primitive Elysium.

In these blues and browns
We can see the truest sorrow and mirth,
Feel the beats in bosom,
Light in eye,
Love in lips.

These words of eroded heart
Are nothing but to solicit
The lost luster of love;
Invocation to drench in unblemished wine
Till the sweetest dawn sprawls golden sun shine.

ALL THAT I TRIED TO MEAN

Requiting heart I tried to mean,
Can my blues touch your green?
Never had I tried to win the race,
I don't have bliss, not even grace.
When the wild dreams fluxed in side,
I couldn't hold it or even hide.
Deluged by myth of a phantom lore,
I took shelter in metaphor;
Deserted soul is a haunted castle.
Where the dreams make din and bustle,
Foams foment in forlorn sea,
Tears try to touch mirth and glee;
These all what I tried to mean
Can my blues touch your green?

HOW CAN I

How can I deny my heart's hidden cry?
How can I defy the ocean of my sigh?

How can I comply with life's low and high?
There is no moon in my midnight sky.

How can I rely on dreams of own eye?
When flower withers and truth becomes lie?

How can I live here, how can I die?
How can I forget your final good bye?

WHEN THE LOVE
WAS GREEN

Tender toes were tossed on sand
On green moor of a distant land,
Twisted tale of a mystic heart
Created pearl of sweetest art.

There on green grass footsteps brown,
Faded towards one village or town,
Budding sweet dreams used to flood,
Throbbing passions in innocent blood.

Touch was divine, kiss was bliss,
Soul was relishing ray of abyss,
Days were lazy and blue were nights,
Dreams were floating in endless heights.

Tears were crystal, warm was mirth,
Friends were sand and pebble and earth,
There in audacious days of teen,
Songs were wrong but love was green.

ETERNAL FLOW

Captivating eye,
Wanton undulating hairs
And innocent lips.

Euphony in voice,
Scintillations in fingers
Fragrance in touch.

She looks like a rose
Or a vase full of tulip
Daisy and lily.

Her countenance glows
In pages of my poetry
Like eternal flow.

TO THE SOUL BENEATH
THE EPITAPH

On your epitaph
Your damsel wailing all day,
Are you listening?

With her blue eyes closed
Your damsel beckoning you,
Are you listening?

On those silent stones
Murmurs of withered petals
Reminiscing you.

How can you be dead?
You must be in sweet slumber
To reincarnate.

How can you be dead?
When heart of such a sweetheart
Beats only for you?

On your epitaph
Your damsel wailing all day,
Are you listening?

———◆◆◆———

REVERIE

Was she a woman?
Or a spell of splendor?
A flamboyant flower?
Or incorporeal flame
Descended from firmament?

Was she a woman?
Or a momentary glint
Over azure emerald
Or mysterious opal,
A captivating euphony
Or metaphor born out of passion?

Was she a woman?
Or an epiphany before
A dreamy eye?
Wafting flickers of a dew?
Soliloquy of a solitary soul?
Monologue of a minstrel?
Or wandering troubadour's sigh?

ONCE UPON A TIME

Once upon a time
When time was teen,
Blue forest of life
Appeared as green.

Once upon a time
When time was sweet,
Melancholy of autumn
Appeared as wit.

Once upon a time
When time was a bird,
Heart was throbbing and
Fancying absurd.

Once upon a time
When time was a steam,
Grey barren reality
Appeared as dream.

Once upon a time
When time was rain,
Touches were tender
And love was insane.

Once upon a time
When time was frost,
Love was found
Yet love was lost.

———◆◆———

SPIRIT OF LOVE

Spirit of love
Floats over the pneuma of night,
Sometimes it blows as breeze,
Sometimes it swirls as dust.

The aura of forest dies out
Under the dense canopy.
Rippling river flows
With the passion of valley,
Fire flies burn in the kingdom of silence.

Spirit of love
White as cloudlets,
Black as deep ocean
Walks over the dead petals of spring.

It comes to me,
Insinuates in my sleepless eye
And entices me by her
Candid countenance.

Touch of her softness
Or music of her voice
Turns my reality surreal.
She holds my hand
And walks like a heavenly angel.

She takes me to the
Fire of stars; dust of galaxies
And constellations of her own.
She nudges the present,
Wails over the past
And kisses the flowers of future;
And from there she takes
A turn towards heaven.
She shows me river of light
Audacious beauty and
Brazen flow of eternal life.

And where the heaven ends
Starts the gateway to hell,
Where the roads are moist and mossy,
Where in every turn and cavern
Glitters the devil's manifesto.

I pass over the hell fire,
The river of blood
And the abodes of specter.

We sit on the cloudlets
To float around the universe,
And she teaches me
To count the stars, touch the planets
Or play with comets and rainbows.

She compels me to look
Beyond the boundaries;
She laughs at our rhetoric
And take out the yellow pages
Of Chronos, where time
Plays rhyme with eternity.

In the horizon of light she
Shows me the dense darkness;
Yet in it flicker
A few distant sparks,
And these never ending dilemmas
Are decorated everywhere.

And there she stands
In the halos of stars and
Storms of nebula
Where everything seems to be in slumber
But moves with utmost sincerity.

And she asks me in this
Ceaseless plurality
Where stands man?
She takes me to the pinnacles of knowledge,
Peaks of paradoxes,
And drags me to the
Realm of introspection.

I feel the futility of a human birth,
The meaninglessness of reality,
Enigmas of change,
And dilemmas of identity.

I feel the nothingness hidden
Inside the being,
Fetters hiding inside freedom,
Or the absurdities in human ethos.

From the fathomless dark
Fire of existential angst
Irks my foundations,
Occult anguish trespasses
All the fences of my tenets and mores,
There is nothing left for me
Except soil and dust.

On that moment of my
Abysmal lament spirit of love
Appears before me.
Spirit of love
White as cloudlets,
Black as ocean,
Caresses me and kisses.
My tears she wipes
And gifts me a vase full of verse
And whispers in my ear
Her sparkling chants
'Take this elixir of eloquence
To the barren soil of earth,
Where time and again
My bards and minstrels
Sprawled delight and mirth;

Put all your ethos
And logic aside
And romanticize heart
With this priceless art'.

Night turns to dawn
I find in my garden lawn
Torn petals and dew.

Spirit of love
Vanquishes with the pneuma of night
Gifting me light of insight
And delight of darkness.

BIRTH OF POETRY

Where sighs of sentimentality die
Poetry begins,
Eloquence plays hide and seek with silence.

There unborn rose oozes with fragrance
Or a dying music dances
Within throbbing heart,
Earnest yearns turn into
Coveted adoration,
Infatuation mutates in devotion.

There enigmas erode the reality,
Dreams start to breed,
Rebellious soul craves for desolation
And rejects the dins of earthly affairs.

There in a weary vase
Love still loves to live
In the guise of a withering petal.

TONIGHT WE MUST NOT SLEEP

Tonight we must dream
Yet we must not sleep,
We must honor
The metaphors, forgotten like forlorn ethos.

Let the camp fire burn,
The forest boughs waft,
Compeers enjoy candid company.

My fair lady
You look no more like a girl,
Even not like a blushed
Damsel hiding inside euphemism,
You seem to be legitimate flower
Of a forbidden vase.

Yet I would like to
Trespass the silence of your soul.

Let us walk and talk
Like two strangers for a while;
I know it is strange to be strangers
Yet we must behave like that.

As the bee knows the flower,
The river knows the ocean
We know each other,
Yet some times it is fair to be unfair.

My fair lady
Look at this moonlit road,
Rocks, pebbles, soil and sand;
I don't want to share sorrows
Or nudge your sweet hand
Yet the forest beckons us.

In azure moorland
A few flickers of golden ray
Irk the drowsy soul,
Tonight we must walk
And be alone for a while.

Tonight we must share our dreams
We must find a shadow
To sit under this endless sky
And to look at our tearless eyes.

Roads diverge, yet the roads meet.
Otherwise how could we be here?
Dreams differ, yet the dreams meet,
Somewhere in some light or shadow.

My fair lady
One day like vanishing dew
I lost you,
Then you bloomed in some garden
Like a dangling daffodil
Or a crimson rose;
Yet I was ever close, never far from you.
You are always in my verse
Even though you are not in my vase.

Tonight we must weep
Yet we must not shed our tears.
Let our past pierce our present and
Agony flow in our blood.

Under this somber sky
Our hearts must depart
Still our eyes must dream for
Yet another birth.
Not in barren heaven but
Here in this sweet earth.

———◆◆———

SYNTHESIS

Let my euphony
Mingle with your symphony
And music be born.

Let all my shadows
Mingle with your twilight light
And colors be born.

Let my earth
Mingle with your sky and
Horizon be born.

Let my death
Mingle with your life and
Poetry be born.

THE LOST LORE

Once upon a time in
Blue sea shore,
Inside the sea shell
Hidden was a lore.

Sea was waving and
Rocks were brown,
It was, far away
From busy town.

Breeze was sweet there
Clouds were gray,
Nights were blue and
Sunny was day.

There used to come
Innocent hand,
Scribbling a love tale
Over the sand.

Love was knocking there
Each other's door,
Hearts were beating in
Sweet implore.

Once upon a time in
Blue sea shore,
Inside the sea shell
Hidden was a lore.

And there were sea gulls
Flying so high,
Kissing the clouds of
Morning sky.

And morning path was
Wet in dew,
Eyes were sharing
Joy and rue.

And there was none but
Two lone hearts,
Tweeting sweetest
Coveted arts.

Art was silent
Like pearl tears,
Days were indolent
Like long years.

Once upon a time in
Blue sea shore
Inside the sea shell
Lost that lore.

Lore of love and
Lore of passion,
Lived and died in
That blue ocean.

———◆◆◆———

BECAUSE THEY MISS YOU

The voice echoes,

River ripples,

Songs reverberate,

Ocean stands still.

Blue yells,

Green wails with brown,

Old laments with new,

It is all because they miss you.

The sparrows are vexed,

Bees are mum,

Buds hide inside petals.

Nights are moonless,

Mornings mourn with dew,

It is all because they miss you.

And nobody can

Rejuvenate them except you.

Winds gone away,

Music fettered in rue,

Flowers lost all glamour,
Colors lost its hue,
It is all because they miss you.
And they really miss you.

———◆◆———

A DAY IN YOUR BAY

Solitude sails me
To the isles of your sea.
In your reticent bay
Passes away my indolent day.

In your rock and stone
I sit and sleep alone,
On your soil and sand
I put my shivering hand.

Your waves splash on my eye,
Your ripples mingle in sigh,
And yes I want to play
With your sand, soil and clay.

WHERE UTILITARIAN HEART DIES

Where all celerities die,
Where life looks like dust under sky,
Where utilitarian heart
Looks back towards pristine art,
There all dreams
Succumb before a tiny rose.

There poetry resurrects,
Love reincarnates,
And hands try to nudge
The blue brown and green
And love springs out of soil
To challenge all unforeseen.

WHY CAN'T WE

Why can't we mingle like
River and the sea?
Why can't we talk like
Rose and the bee?
Why can't we be like
Light and the shadow?
Why can't we kiss like
Sky and the meadow?
Why can't we sing like
Spring and the shower?
Why can't we dance like
Butterfly and flower?
Why can't we nudge like
Soil and the sand?
Why can't we touch sorrows
With each other's hand?
Why can't we rest in nest
Like a pair of dove?
Why can't we eternally
Indulge in love?

SUMIT DATTA

A PHANTOM WALK

In moonlit night
When stars nudge the cloudlets
Spills the music of heaven.

Forlorn forest road
Undulates in lazy breeze;
Soul of silent lake
Beckons the spirit of love.

I walk with her
Entwined by her sweetness.
Embraced by her warmth,
Maddened by her fragrance,
Enchanted by her voice.

I walk and walk with her
Until I reach the horizon
And I lose my destiny.

I see her face
Flooded in moonlight,
Her lips, her innocent blush
Her rippling hair,
Her eyes with a burning stare.

The wind plays with her,
The mist kisses her hands,
And the shadows decorate her
Like a blooming flower.

My soul burns to exchange the fire,
My dreams knock the window of reality,
My eyes ooze with tears of ecstasy.

I sit with her
Under the stars and cloud,
I talk with her
In the language of zephyr,
I walk with her
In the forest of life
And when we reached nowhere

I see tears flowing
From her eyes,
And she tells that she died
Long back in the soil of earth.

THAT UNFORGETTABLE TOUCH

Soft yet piercing,

Inundating every corner of vein.

Ephemeral yet eternal,

And yes, I hide it inside deepest

Cavern of my heart.

Like vexing ripples

Or beckoning reverberation

It erodes every sand and stone of my soul.

In disquieting desolation or

Sweet moments of melancholy

It steps over my heart.

That unforgettable touch

Which still spills upon me

The thrills of light and

Cradle of shadows

Makes the tears of life

To flow into the bay of love.

LOVE LINES – 4

When the river flows,
It brings your ripples to me, closer and close.

When the breeze blows,
It brings your fragrance to me, closer and close.

When blooms the rose,
It brings your blush to me, closer and close.

When midnight moon glows,
It brings your delight to me, closer and close.

All the life's highs and lows,
Bring to me your saga, closer and close.

And all those heavenly and earthly shows,
Put me in deep sleep with your dreams, why, who knows?

BLUES WITHIN THE BLUE

Deep in the ocean
There lived mermaid of my dream
In eternal blues.

She swam and played with
Silver ripples and bubbles,
Sand, stones and pebbles.

She walked on the weeds,
Talked with the buds and danced
With swirls of the fish.

One day on shoreline
When I was trudging under
Sedating moon shine

She nudged my fingers
And gave me a look that shook
All doors of my heart.

By magic of night
Or audacious bliss, she
Promised me a kiss,

Beguiled by beauty
Or charmed by innocence,
Deep, I was enticed.

I followed her trails
Under the azure ocean,
Her reels and ripples.

She passed the caverns,
Mossy stones, deadly corners,
Whirling, bubbling vents.

Near came her castle,
Inside misty ray less realm
Glittered golden stones.

Its glare and splendor
Irked my eye and left me vexed;
I stood motionless.

I went to enter
And stood by the fancy entrance,
My brain was in trance.

My hands were shaking
Senses sprinted and heart galloped
As I passed the gate.

And that was my fate,
I encountered the next gate
Where they made me wait.

And waited I there
With flare in heart, eye filled tears
From dawn to the dusk.

And that was my task
Overcome the endless fence
From dawn to the dusk.

My limbs turned weary,
Senses turned numb, as I stood
Near colossal gate.

With my hopeless fate
I saw glint and heard music
Flowing from within.

Colors were dancing
Flowers floating on waves
As I looked from out

There stood, as I doubt.
Between me and my mermaid
Limit less gulf and void.

———◆———

ENDURANCE

Lunar luminescence on lone land,
Silence puts her tranquil hand,
Silver ripple on amber lake
With the white fog makes handshake,
Unknown bird's wings flap in dark
Before the eye dies old skylark.

Drops of dew on withered leaf,
Melting heart in solacing grief.

Moments evanescent, time in cruel,
Rust all in dust precious jewel,
Nothing endures, but I see
Walking on moonlight you and me;
Hypnotized all, I am awake,
Near the dark and silent lake.

BIRTH OF AESTHETICS

Million moon's boon and delight
Rippling with sincere radiance,
In the sweet solace of that prized eyes,
Indolence of that delicate glance.

The genesis of adoration in brain
Yet agony torments the heart,
Soul slips in indulgence of innocence,
Trances in romance and art.

Birth of a love tale escalates in ecstasy
Finishes in the anguish of sleepless nights,
Yet carrying these silly fairytales
The barren heart reaches unattainable heights.

Give me that cup of heavenly wine,
That divine touch, blush and shyness,
Invented in the age of savagery, or aesthetics
Of meaningless rituals on terrestrial dryness,

Without wallowing in love, who on earth
Can chant the highest hymn?
Landscape of life will turn ever grey,
Poetry will putrefy in degenerated rhyme.

THE LOTUS LADY

Lotus lady under sweet shadows of maples
Musing around,
Lazy breeze captivated by
Dazzling elegance forgot to blow.

Lotus lady in sincere fun
With the lake ripples.
Sunlight, delighted by
The elfin charm professing
The prudence of that countenance.

Lotus lady,
Her tiptoeing toes
Tossing on my heart,
Drenched hands caressing
The soul to solacing hypnosis.

Lotus lady walks away
In deep wilderness;
The lost image sublimates
Somewhere in me
Like an incessant mirage.

THE MIDNIGHT AURA

The midnight aura tiding
In the terrible mind storm;
Scream of my deadliest dream
Springing from the steadfast
Desire's unquelled rebellion
To break murky barriers
Between you and me.

The creed, faith, customs
Hide their face before the
Mystic countenance.
The placid innocence of
Ripening lips, the moonlight look,
The tweeting talk,
The majestic walk.

My heart stops beating,
Ecstasy entices the sense;
O angelic beauty, how can I tell?
I want to be your eternal minstrel.

TRANCE

Hallucinating you, in the
Soothing twilight softness,
In the euphony of weary bird's
Melodious melancholy.

Illusioning you, in the
Morning dew's azure hue,
Dillusioning you, in the
Moisture of my eye.
Your enigmatic image
Deluded me like a disquieting mirage.

Let me be inundated by the flow
And live with these steadfast ceaseless glow;
Let me take refuge in these whims,
So that I can sleep with these absurd dreams.

DREAMS IN DESOLATION

Hold this fugitive frenzy
Near your solacing face,
Quell the rebellion of unquenched crave
By your soothing hand's placid embrace.

Delirious I am, the squalling outcries
Rampaging the sweetness of my sleep;
Body needs to be nestled, soul kissed,
Heart caressed with touches, gentle and deep.

O beguiling beauty turn these
Tumultuous passions to flawless adoration,
So I can love you ceaselessly
With heart's deepest veneration.

———•◆•———

STOPPED BY A SYMBOL
ETCHED ON A ROCK

Noxious intoxication of night
Flooded with delirious moonlight,
Allusion of an elusive hand
Impressed upon the eroding sand.

Lament of wanton breeze
Under the woods put on siege,
Lore of Gnostic nous
Floats in the bricks of broken house.

Time stands still in sky,
The galaxies relax, the stars die,
Desolation induces the sense
To deep, deeper, deepest repentance.

The dins, bustles, the civilized roar
Washed away by dark seashore,
The pristine quests of mankind
Haunt the tranquil mind.

Life like a drop of dew
Vanquishes; old reincarnates in new
Why then yearns and cravings govern the heart?
Why love, loftiest; almost lost an art?

The fuzzy symbolism of logic
Loses meaning before divine magic,
Imperial cults shatter in the long run,
Turn to absurd colossal fun.

Your sweet glance like a divine dove
Ignites my night like theophany of love,
Here on these grains of sand,
I see the etch and imprint of your hand.

When the roars are over in dark
I see the sea of immortal spark,
I lament before your eye,
I know my dreams are about to die.

Gnosis buried under stone,
Heart's outcries lament in lone,
Beauty deserted the fossilized soul,
Tears even can't play its pristine role.

Let them live in day, us in night,

Let then live in joy, us in plight,

The Day of Judgment will solve the mystery,

The gems of soul will ornate the history.

———◆◆◆———

TWINKLING TEARS - HAIKU

Twinkling tears break the
Symphony of your silence
And mingle in sigh.

RELICS - HAIKU

Tears deluging me,
I am excavating the
Relics of lost love.

WONDERLAND - HAIKU

I trudge on dry sand,
Your heart is my wonderland,
Deny not, my love.

A WISH - HAIKU

O matchless beauty,
Let me touch blues of your sky,
And sail on your sea.

SUMIT DATTA

EPIPHANY - HAIKU

Truth will reign my heart
The moment you nudge my art,
All my lies will die.

LANGUAGE OF LOVE
- HAIKU

Language of love

Does not need any phonetics,

Semantics guide heart.

ROMANCE - HAIKU

Near the stormy bay
Romance of river with sea
Puts the waves in trance.

LET IT BE - HAIKU

Let rose decorate
Your eye, poetry your ear
And music your soul.

A MOMENT OF SILENCE
- HAIKU

Tiny drops of tears
Tossed up like pearly crystal,
Silencing all songs.

HIDDEN TREASURES
- HAIKU

Inside the whirls of
Your sigh, I try to find out
Piece of tiny pearl.

IMPLORE - HAIKU

First let me trespass
The arcadia of your heart,
Then prosecute me.

DIVINE AGONY - HAIKU

Your toes on my heart
Resurrects agony, yet
It never hurts me.

TOUCH OF HYPNOSIS
- HAIKU

Touch of hypnosis

Compels dreams to sublimate

In blues of your eye.

WHEN LYRICS DIE OUT
- HAIKU

When lyrics die out
Rise sentimental ballads
From ocean of blues.

———————

DREAM OF A SPRING
- HAIKU

A dying daisy

Kissing the wings of a bee

With dream of a spring.

CRYSTAL TEARS - HAIKU

From tender eyelash
Splash few drops of crystal tears,
Drenching my dry earth.

SUMIT DATTA

FRAGRANCE OF HEART
- HAIKU

A trodden jasmine
Filled the firmament of night
With fragrance of heart.

SOLILOQUY - HAIKU

Sweet soliloquy

Soothes sigh of a squalling soul

Smoothens solitude.